THE CRAZY JOKE BOOK

BOOK

STRIKES BACK!

Janet Rogers

Illustrated by Robert Nixon

RED FOX

THE CRAZY JOKE BOOK STRIKES BACK
A RED FOX BOOK 978 1 849 41858 4

First published in Great Britain by Beaver Books,
an imprint of Random House Children's Publishers UK
A Random House Group Company

Beaver Books edition published 1985
Red Fox edition published 2012

1 3 5 7 9 10 8 6 4 2

The Random House Group Limited supports the Forest Stewardship Council
(FSC®), the leading international forest certification organization. Our books
carrying the FSC label are printed on FSC®-certified paper. FSC is the only
forest certification scheme endorsed by the leading environmental organiza-
tions, including Greenpeace. Our paper procurement policy can be found at
www.randomhouse.co.uk/environment.

Set in Century Schoolbook by JH Graphics Ltd, Reading, Berks

Red Fox Books are published by Random House Publishers UK,
61–63 Uxbridge Road, London W5 5SA

www.randomhousechildrens.co.uk
www.randomhouse.co.uk

Addresses for companies within The Random House Group Limited can be
found at: www.randomhouse.co.uk/offices.htm

THE RANDOM HOUSE GROUP Limited Reg. No. 954009

A CIP catalogue record for this book is available from the British Library.

Printed and bound by CPI Group (UK) Ltd, Croydon, CR0 4YY

Introduction

The oldest joke I know is when Eve asked Adam, 'Do you love me?' and he answered, 'Who else?' Although I haven't actually been around since the time of Adam and Eve, I have been writing joke books for a long, long time. First there was *The Crazy Joke Book,* then *More Crazy Jokes,* followed by *Even Crazier Jokes,* and of course *The Craziest Joke Book Of All.*

Following in the Rogers' tradition, my nieces and nephews got together and decided that they knew some even funnier crazy jokes. At first I thought this was impossible, but to prove me wrong they have produced THE CRAZY JOKE BOOK STRIKES BACK! Every one of my twenty-six nieces and nephews has presented me with their top twenty favourite jokes. Here are the twenty different categories:

1. Favourite Shaggy Dog Story

2. Favourite Wisecrack

3. Favourite Knock Knock

4. Favourite Animal Joke

5. Favourite Monster Joke

6. Favourite Potty Poem

Because this is really their book, my nieces and nephews are only allowing me one joke of my own. So here's my favourite joke at the moment!

A very weak and weedy-looking man went into a bar for a drink. Behind the bar was a most peculiar-looking man with a hump on his back, like Quasimodo. Nudging the man next to him, the weak-looking man said:
'I say, look at the size of the hump on that barman's back.'
The man stood up, grabbed him by the lapels and lifted him high into the air, saying:

6

'That barman happens to be my brother!'

'I say,' said the other man, 'doesn't that hump suit him!'

From now on, things can only get better as THE CRAZY JOKE BOOK STRIKES BACK!

THE CRAZY JOKE BOOK STRIKES BACK! is dedicated to my twenty-six nieces and nephews – thirteen girls and thirteen boys – who have supplied the jokes for this book. They are:

ANNIE	NIGEL
BEN	OLIVE
CAROL	PAUL
DARREN	QUEENIE
ELIZABETH	ROGER
FRANCIS	SALLY
GEORGIE*	THOMAS
HARVEY	UNA
ISADORA**	VICTOR
JAMES	WINCY
KATY	X***
LOUIS	YVONNE
MATILDA	ZENO****

   * Her name is really Georgina, but she likes to be called Georgie.

  ** Named after a famous American dancer called Isadora Duncan.

 *** This is my shy nephew; he wants to remain anonymous.

**** Named after a fifth-century Roman Emperor because they share the same birthdate.

Annie's top twenty

Annie's favourite shaggy dog story

A man burst into a dentist's surgery waving a gun in the air. He pointed the gun at the dentist's head and said:

'I want you to take all my teeth out!'

'But there's nothing wrong with your teeth,' exclaimed the dentist.

'I don't care,' said the man, 'I want them all out.'

'I'll just give you an injection,' said the dentist, trying to remain calm.

'I don't want an injection,' said the man, 'I don't want gas, I don't want anything. Just pull them out.'

'But if you don't have an anaesthetic the pain will be absolutely unbearable.'

'I don't care,' said the man, 'just pull them out one at a time and pull them out slowly.'

The dentist was very nervous, but the gun was pointed at him so he pulled the teeth out one by one, without any anaesthetic. When he had pulled the final tooth out, the man leapt out of the chair and pulled the trigger of the gun! Out popped a flag which said: 'BANG!'

'April Fool!' laughed the man. 'I only came to buy a toothbrush!'

Annie's favourite wisecrack

'I named my horse "Radish". Now I can say: "Look, here's my horse Radish."'

Annie's favourite knock knock

Knock, knock.
Who's there?
Annie.
Annie who?
Annie body here going to answer the door?

Annie's favourite animal joke

BEN: *I'm going to keep this skunk under my bed.*
IVY: But what about the smell?
BEN: *He'll just have to get used to that.*

Annie's favourite monster joke

Why did the two cyclops fight?
They could never see eye-to-eye over anything.

Annie's favourite potty poem

'Your teeth are like the stars,' he said,
And pressed her hand so white.
He spoke the truth, for like the stars,
Her teeth came out at night.

Annie's favourite doctor doctor joke

'*Doctor, doctor, there's something wrong with my stomach.*'
'Keep your coat buttoned up and nobody will notice.'

Annie's favourite waiter waiter joke

WAITER: *I have boiled tongue, fried liver, and frogs' legs.*

CUSTOMER: Don't bother me with your troubles, just get me a menu.

Annie's favourite daft definition

IMPECCABLE – Something that chickens cannot eat.

Annie's favourite elephant joke

Why do elephants wear green felt hats?
So they can walk across snooker tables without being seen.

Annie's favourite graffiti

LIGHTNING NEVER STRIKES TWICE IN THE SAME PLACE
No, if it strikes once, the same place isn't there any more!

Annie's favourite limerick

There was a young fellow from Glasgow
Whose party proved quite a fiasco.
At eight-thirty, about,
The lights all went out
Through a lapse on the part of the gas co.

Annie's favourite ghost joke

What is a ghost's favourite dessert?
Strawberries and scream.

Annie's favourite school joke

ZENO: *I got a bad school report because I got zero in one subject.*
QUEENIE: Just one subject? What was it?
ZENO: *Attendance.*

Annie's favourite funny book title

The Big Party by Maud D. Merrier

Annie's favourite misprint

HOUSE FOR SALE. Within striking distance of local engineering works.

Annie's favourite pun joke

What did the parents say when their son wanted to play the drums?
'Beat it!'

Annie's favourite family joke

MRS BROWN: *Your son thinks he's a cat. You ought to have him seen to.*

MRS JONES: I did, and the vet says he's in perfect health.

Annie's favourite riddle

What's the quickest way to cure double vision?
Shut one eye!

Annie's top favourite joke of all time

'*Mother won a saucepan in a competition.*'
'That's what you call pot luck!'

Ben's top twenty

Ben's favourite shaggy dog story

One lunchtime a workman sat down with his workmates to eat his lunch, and got out a box of sandwiches. When he looked inside he found that they were sardine and lettuce sandwiches.

'Oh dear,' he said, 'I don't really like sardine and lettuce sandwiches, but never mind.'

The next day the same workman sat down to lunch and opened his box of sandwiches – sardine and lettuce again.

'Oh dear,' said the man. 'More sardine and lettuce.'

The next day exactly the same thing happened. One of his workmates said:

'Why don't you tell your wife that you don't like sardine and lettuce sandwiches?'

'That wouldn't make any difference,' said the man. 'She doesn't make the sandwiches – I do.'

Ben's favourite wisecrack

If it takes an apple a day to keep the doctor away, what does it take to get rid of the nurse?

Ben's favourite knock knock

Knock, knock.
Who's there?
Ben.
Ben who?
Ben Dover and touch the floor.

Ben's favourite animal joke

MATILDA: *There's something I hate about my dog.*
ELIZABETH: What's that?
MATILDA: *Every time there's a thunderstorm he hides under the bed.*
ELIZABETH: What's wrong with that?
MATILDA: *There isn't enough room for me.*

Ben's favourite monster joke

Where do vampires keep their money?
In blood banks.

Ben's favourite potty poem

Mary had a little lamb,
Her father shot it dead.
And now it goes to school with her
Between two chunks of bread.

Ben's favourite doctor doctor joke

'Doctor, doctor, those strength pills you gave me just aren't doing any good.'
'Why not?'
'I can't get the top off the bottle.'

Ben's favourite waiter waiter joke

'Waiter, waiter, have you smoked salmon?'
'No, I've only ever smoked a pipe.'

Ben's favourite daft definition

SKELETON – Someone who went on a diet and forgot to say 'when'.

Ben's favourite graffiti

IF EVERYONE LETS YOU DOWN, THERE'S ONE THING YOU CAN ALWAYS COUNT ON – YOUR FINGERS

Ben's favourite limerick

A major, with wonderful force,
Called out in Hyde Park for a horse.
All the flowers looked round
But no horse could be found;
So he just rhododendron, of course.

Ben's favourite elephant joke

Where can you buy ancient elephants?
At a mammoth sale.

Ben's favourite ghost joke

Why do demons and ghouls get on so well?
Because demons are a ghoul's best friend.

Ben's favourite school joke

SON: *Were you good at sport when you were at school, Dad?*
DAD: I shall never forget the time I ran fifteen hundred metres in ten seconds. And if I ever find out who put those wasps in my shorts, I'll kill them!

Ben's favourite family joke

MOTHER: *My Dilbert's taking ten 'O' levels this summer.*
FRIEND: Oh, will he be having a coach?
MOTHER: *No, just a new bike if he gets them.*

Ben's favourite funny book title

Improve Your Target Shooting by Mr Completely

Ben's favourite misprint

'Then one of the new Labour MPs rushed across the floor and shook a clenched fish in the Prime Minister's face.'

Daily Telegraph

Ben's favourite pun joke

A pilot was flying along in a small plane one day when suddenly the plane broke down. Quickly he ejected and parachuted down to safety in the jungle. Unfortunately he landed in a cannibal's cooking pot. Fishing him out, the cannibal chief demanded:
     'What's this flier doing in my soup?'

Ben's favourite riddle

What happens when you cross an octopus with a turkey?
The whole family can have a leg at Christmas.

Ben's top favourite joke of all time

What is a crick?
The noise a Japanese camera makes.

Carol's top twenty

Carol's favourite shaggy dog story

A little boy was told that he needed glasses and was sent along to the optician's to have his eyes tested. The optician sat him down in front of a big chart, which was covered in letters.

'Now,' said the optician, 'cover your right eye with your right hand and read the chart with your left eye.'

But the little boy didn't know which was his right hand and which was his left.

'All right,' said the optician, 'if you find it easier, cover your left eye with your left hand and read the chart.'

The little boy still did not know which eye to cover. The optician was a very kind man, so to make things really easy, he took a cardboard box and cut a small hole on one side. He then put the box over the little boy's head. The optician was just about to ask him to read the chart when he noticed that the little boy was crying.

'Why are you crying?' asked the optician.

'Because', sobbed the little boy, 'I wanted a pair of metal frames like my brother.'

Carol's favourite wisecrack

'My friend's got a face like a million dollars – all green and wrinkled!'

Carol's favourite knock knock

Knock, knock.
Who's there?
Carol.
Carol who?
Carol go if you put petrol in it!

Carol's favourite animal joke

Which animals have their eyes closest together?
The ones with the smallest heads!

Carol's favourite monster joke

CAROL: *Yesterday I took my boyfriend to see 'The Monster Strikes Again' at the cinema.*
YVONNE: What was he like?
CAROL: *Oh, about nine foot tall, with two heads and a bolt through each neck. Really, really ugly.*
YVONNE: I don't mean your boyfriend – what was the monster in the film like?

Carol's favourite potty poem

Mary had a little lamb
(You've heard this tale before),
But did you know she passed her plate
And had a little more?

Carol's favourite doctor doctor joke

'Doctor, doctor, I feel like a yo-yo.'
'Sit down, sit down, sit down.'

Carol's favourite waiter waiter joke

'Waiter, waiter, there's a twig in my soup!'
'Yes, Madam, we have branches everywhere.'

Carol's favourite daft definition

OYSTER – What you shout when you want someone to lift your mother up.

Carol's favourite graffiti

PHOTOGRAPHS NEVER DO ME JUSTICE
It's mercy you want, not justice!

Carol's favourite limerick

There was a young lady from Crete
Who was so exceedingly neat,
When she got out of bed
She stood on her head
To make sure of not soiling her feet.

Carol's favourite elephant joke

Why can't two elephants swim together?
Because they've only got one pair of trunks
between them.

Carol's favourite ghost joke

What goes through a wall saying 'Oob oob'?
A ghost going backwards.

Carol's favourite school joke

TEACHER: *What can you tell me about nitrates?*
CAROL: They're cheaper than day rates, Miss.

Carol's favourite family joke

MOTHER: *Now you've finished your lunch you can
say grace.*
CAROL: OK – 'Thanks for the lunch, Lord.'
MOTHER: *That wasn't much of a grace, Carol.*
CAROL: Well, it wasn't much of a lunch.

Carol's favourite funny book title

My Favourite Sweets by Annie Seedball

Carol's favourite misprint

'The state trumpeters played a funfair as the
Prince and Princess of Wales entered the hall.'
Yorkshire Post

Carol's favourite pun joke

I bought some of those new paper knickers. I don't like them though – they're tearable.

Carol's favourite riddle

What happened to the snake that caught cold?
She adder viper nose.

Carol's top favourite joke of all time

How do you play Russian Roulette in India?
You play the flute with six cobras around you, and one of them is deaf!

Darren's top twenty

Darren's favourite shaggy dog story

Some members of an African tribe found a beautiful throne in the jungle. It seemed to be made of pure gold, and they carried it back to their village and built a special grass hut to keep it in. The hut was guarded day and night, and no one was allowed to enter. At the end of the rainy season, the chief went into the hut to find the throne all covered with green mould. He was very upset, but his wife touched him on the shoulder and said gently, 'It just goes to show, dear, people who live in grass houses shouldn't store thrones.'

Darren's favourite wisecrack

'Is that your face or are you still wearing a gas
    mask?'

Darren's favourite knock knock

Knock, knock.
Who's there?
Dismay.
Dismay who?
Dismay be a joke, but it doesn't make me laugh.

Darren's favourite animal joke

What did the cowboy say when its dog fell over a cliff?
'Dawg gone.'

Darren's favourite monster joke

Why did the cyclops give up teaching?
It only had one pupil.

Darren's favourite potty poem

A man stood on a bridge one night,
His lips were all a-quiver.
He gave a cough,
His leg fell off
And floated down the river.

Darren's favourite doctor doctor joke

'Doctor, doctor, I think I'm a clock.'
'Don't get wound up about it.'

Darren's favourite waiter waiter joke

'Waiter, waiter, there's a dead fly in my soup.'
'Yes, sir – it's the heat that kills them.'

Darren's favourite daft definition

TORTOISE – What the teacher did in school.

Darren's favourite graffiti

*YOU THINK YOU'VE GOT TROUBLES – MY
SUNDIAL IS SLOW*

Darren's favourite limerick

A steeplechase jockey called Ron
A most obstinate mare sat upon.
When half round the course
'That's enough!' said the horse,
And she stopped while the rider went on.

Darren's favourite elephant joke

Why do elephants wear slippers?
So that they can sneak up on mice without being
   heard.

Darren's favourite ghost joke

What do you call a ghost doctor?
A surgical spirit.

Darren's favourite school joke

TEACHER: *If I had fifty apples in one hand and sixty in the other, what would I have?*
PUPIL: Extremely big hands, Miss!

Darren's favourite family joke

'My dad makes faces all day long.'
'Why?'
'He works in a clock factory.'

Darren's favourite funny book title

End of the Week by Gladys Friday

Darren's favourite misprint

'We apologize for the error in last week's paper in which we stated that Mr Harold Goodbody was a defective in the police force. This was a typographical error. We meant, of course, that Mr Goodbody was a detective in the police farce, and we are sorry for any embarrassment caused.'

Kingston News

Darren's favourite pun joke

What did the beaver say as it left the tree?
'It's been nice gnawing you.'

Darren's favourite riddle

What sits on the bottom of the sea and shakes?
A nervous wreck.

Darren's top favourite joke of all time

'This cake tastes funny.'
'Well I followed the recipe exactly. It said separate two eggs, so I put one on the kitchen table and the other out in the garden.'

Elizabeth's top twenty

Elizabeth's favourite shaggy dog story

An American was visiting Australia. His Australian host was showing him around the country. First they went to Sydney harbour.

'Do you like our Opera House?' said the host.

'Very nice,' said the American, 'but we've got opera houses twice that size in America.'

'What about our lovely parks?' asked the Australian.

'Yes, quite picturesque, but we have parks four times the size in America,' said the American.

'What about our unusual bridges?' asked the Australian.

'Our bridges are much longer and stronger than yours,' said the American.

Just at that moment a kangaroo hopped by.

'I must admit one thing, though,' said the American, 'your fleas are a little larger than ours.'

Elizabeth's favourite wisecrack

'Didn't you hear me pounding on your ceiling during your party last night?'
'Oh, that's all right. We were making a lot of noise ourselves.'

Elizabeth's favourite knock knock

Knock, knock.
Who's there?
Percy.
Percy who?
Persevere and you may find out.

Elizabeth's favourite animal joke

What do you call a rabbit that inspects holes?
A borough surveyor.

Elizabeth's favourite monster joke

How can you tell when a mummy is angry?
It flips its lid.

Elizabeth's favourite potty poem

Early to bed
And early to rise
Makes you feel stupid
And gives you red eyes.

Elizabeth's favourite doctor doctor joke

'Doctor, doctor, I feel like a strawberry.'
'You *are* in a jam, aren't you?'

Elizabeth's favourite waiter waiter joke

'Waiter, waiter, does the orchestra play requests?'
'Yes, sir.'
*'Well, tell them to play cards until I've finished my
    meal.'*

Elizabeth's favourite daft definition

WHOSE – Where a Scotsman lives.

Elizabeth's favourite graffiti

*A BIRD IN THE HAND IS A NUISANCE
WHEN YOU WANT TO PICK YOUR NOSE*

Elizabeth's favourite limerick

An incompetent sailor named Scott
Tried crossing the channel by yacht.
A storm blew him off course,
So he tapped out in Morse:

. . . — — . . .

Elizabeth's favourite elephant joke

Which is stronger, a snail or an elephant?
A snail, because it carries a house and an
elephant only carries a trunk.

Elizabeth's favourite ghost joke

Which ghost appears on the front of glamour magazines?
The cover ghoul.

Elizabeth's favourite school joke

TEACHER: *Now, I will use my hat to represent the planet Venus. Are there any questions?*
PUPIL: Yes, sir. Is Venus inhabited?

Elizabeth's favourite family joke

SON: *Mum, do people really come from dust?*
MOTHER: In a way, yes.
SON: *And when they go, do they return to dust?*
MOTHER: Sort of – why?
SON: *Well, there's someone either coming or going under my bed.*

Elizabeth's favourite funny book title

I'm Absolutely Certain by R. U. Sure

Elizabeth's favourite misprint

'A small fire in a coal shed at 3 Arne Lane, Maidenhead, was put out by firemen on Friday afternoon. Mrs P. Colverson was the pianist.'
Provincial paper

Elizabeth's favourite pun joke

How do you start a pudding race?
Sago.

Elizabeth's favourite riddle

What is the quickest way to get to the railway station?
Run like mad.

Elizabeth's top favourite joke of all time

'Mum, I've just knocked over the ladder that was against the side of the house.'

'Run and tell your father. I'm busy at the moment.'

'I think he knows already, Mum. He was at the top of the ladder when I knocked it over.'

Can I cheat and put in one extra favourite?

'Mum, Dad's just fallen off the roof.'
'I know, dear. I just saw him go past the window.'

Francis's top twenty

Francis's favourite shaggy dog story

Mrs Brown was upset one day when she couldn't get her fire to light. She tried using paper and sticks, firelighters and every trick she could think of, but still the coal would not catch light. She was muttering angrily about the new coal she'd bought not being any good, when her daughter came in.

'Don't worry, Mum,' she said, 'I'll fix it.' She went down to the cellar and brought up a bucket of the previous winter's coal, set to, and soon had a cheery blaze going. 'You see, Mum,' she said, 'there's no fuel like an old fuel.'

Francis's favourite wisecrack

'Can you lend me 10p? I want to call a friend.'
'Here's 20p. Call all of them.'

Francis's favourite knock knock

Knock, knock.
Who's there?
Francis.
Francis who?
Francisn't the capital of Paris, you idiot!

Francis's favourite animal joke

Did you hear about the jellyfish? It set.

Francis's favourite monster joke

Which is the monster's favourite ballet?
Swamp Lake.

Francis's favourite potty poem

Mother heard her children scream
So she pushed them in the stream,
Saying, as she pushed the third,
'Children should be seen, *not* heard.'

Francis's favourite doctor doctor joke

'Doctor, doctor, I can't stop myself stealing things.'
'Have you taken anything for it?'

Francis's favourite waiter waiter joke

'Waiter, waiter, I'm in a hurry. Will my pancake be long?'
'No, sir, it will be round.'

Francis's favourite daft definition

FELON – Dropped on from above.

Francis's favourite graffiti

IRISH TREETS, MELT IN THE PACKET NOT IN YOUR HAND

Francis's favourite ghost joke

Which ghost made friends with the three bears?
Ghouldilocks.

Francis's favourite limerick

There once was a gnu in the zoo
Who tired of the same daily view.
To seek a new sight
He stole out one night,
And where he went gnobody gnu.

Francis's favourite elephant joke

INQUIRER: *I want to put an advertisement in your weekly newspaper.*

TELEPHONIST: Is it to go in the small ads?

INQUIRER: *Oh, goodness, no! I want to sell an elephant.*

Francis's favourite school joke

A chemistry teacher was giving a demonstration about acids and how they work. He took a glass container of acid and dropped a one-pound coin into it.

'I've dropped a coin into this acid,' he said. 'Now will it dissolve?'

'No, sir, it won't,' said a boy.

'That's right,' said the teacher, 'but how did you know?'

'Because if that one-pound coin was going to dissolve, I know you would never have dropped it in.'

Francis's favourite family joke

A couple's happy married life was nearly ruined by old Aunt Tabitha. For ten years she lived with them, and she was always very bad tempered and made life unbearable for them. Eventually she died.

On the way back from the funeral, the husband confessed to his wife: 'Darling, if I didn't love you so much, I don't think I could have put up with having your Aunt Tabitha living with us all those years.'

'*My* Aunt Tabitha?' cried the wife. 'I always thought she was *your* Aunt Tabitha!'

Francis's favourite funny book title

The Angry Lion by Claudia Armoff

Francis's favourite misprint

'The bride was gowned in white and silk lace. The colour scheme of the bridesmaids' gowns and flowers was punk.'

Woking Herald

Francis's favourite riddle

What has twenty-two legs and two wings but cannot fly?
A football team.

Francis's favourite pun joke

'What kind of nuts would you like?'
'Cashew.'
'Bless you! Now, what kind of nuts would you like?'

Francis's top favourite joke of all time

What is bright red and stupid?
A blood clot.

Georgie's top twenty

Georgie's favourite shaggy dog story

A young boy had the reputation for not being very bright, and people often used to play tricks on him to try and make him look a fool. Many people got a lot of fun out of putting two coins in his hand – a fifty pence piece and a pound coin – and telling him to take his pick of the two. The boy always took the fifty pence piece.

A kind hearted woman asked him one day if he didn't know the difference, pointing out that although the pound coin was smaller, it was actually worth twice as much.

'Yes, I know that,' said the boy, 'but if I took the pound coin, they wouldn't try the trick out on me any more.'

Georgie's favourite wisecrack

'I'll have you know, I've got the face of a sixteen-year-old.'
'Well, give it back. You're getting it all wrinkled.'

Georgie's favourite knock knock

Knock, knock.
Who's there?
Wendy.
Wendy who?
Wendy joke is over, you'd better laugh or else!

Georgie's favourite animal joke

How did the Egyptian worm catch a cold?
It caught it from its mummy.

Georgie's favourite monster joke
What do you call a clean, kind-hearted monster?
A failure.

Georgie's favourite potty poem

Billy, in one of his nice new sashes,
Fell in the fire and was burnt to ashes;
Now, although the room grows chilly,
I haven't the heart to poke poor Billy.

Georgie's favourite doctor doctor joke

'Doctor, doctor, I feel like a spoon.'
'Sit down and don't stir.'

Georgie's favourite waiter waiter joke
'Waiter, waiter, I can't eat this. Bring the manager.'
'He won't eat it either, sir.'

Georgie's favourite daft definition
HOLLOW – An empty greeting.

Georgie's favourite graffiti

IF IT WASN'T FOR VENETIAN BLINDS IT WOULD BE CURTAINS FOR ALL OF US

Georgie's favourite limerick

A girl we all know as Beat
Is so unusually neat
She washes all day
To keep microbes away,
And wears rubber gloves just to eat.

Georgie's favourite family joke

What happened to the two kangaroos that got married?
They lived hoppily ever after.

Georgie's favourite elephant joke

How do you tell an elephant from a monster?
A monster never remembers.

Georgie's favourite ghost joke

What did one ghost say to another?
'I'm sorry, but I just don't believe in people.'

Georgie's favourite school joke

Georgie came home from school one day and said to her mother,
   'Mum, is the stuff in that yellow bottle in the cupboard hair lacquer?'
   'No, dear,' said her mother. 'That's super glue.'
   'No wonder I couldn't get my beret off at school today.'

Georgie's favourite funny book title

Nothing's Ever Right by Mona Lott

Georgie's favourite misprint

'The Misses Vivian, Lily May and Dorothy Smith are spending some time at the home of their mother, Mrs Agatha Smith. This is the first time the village has had the pleasure of seeing the girls in the altogether in ten years.'
                    Lancashire Evening Telegraph

Georgie's favourite pun joke

What is Father Christmas's wife's name?
Mary Christmas.

Georgie's favourite riddle

How do you keep an idiot in suspense?
I'll tell you tomorrow.

Georgie's top favourite joke of all time

NEWSPAPER BOY: *Do you know, there's a man on my paper round who has thirty-five daily papers. I have to stagger with them to his place every day.*

GIRL: He must be very intelligent to read all that lot.

NEWSPAPER BOY: *Oh, he doesn't read them. He owns a pet shop.*

Harvey's top twenty

Harvey's favourite shaggy dog story

A gambler in a casino won £2000 one night. When he got home he put the money under his pillow, and said to his wife, 'In the morning I'm going to buy you a diamond ring.' He was so excited about his win that he couldn't sleep, and got up and went back to the casino with the money to try and win more. But unfortunately he lost it all.

In the morning his wife woke him up and said, 'Let's go and buy that diamond ring.' The gambler slid his hand under the pillow and sighed. 'Go back to sleep,' he said, 'I don't feel two grand.'

Harvey's favourite wisecrack

'Why were you late for school?'
'There are eight of us in my family and the alarm was only set for seven.'

Harvey's favourite knock knock

Knock, knock.
Who's there?
Harvey.
Harvey who?
Harvey going to have lunch? I'm hungry.

Harvey's favourite animal joke

Why is a kettle like an animal?
Because it is a water otter.

Harvey's favourite monster joke

*'Mummy, Mummy, why do I keep going round in
circles?'*
'Be quiet, or I'll nail your other foot to the floor.'

Harvey's favourite potty poem

The night was growing dark and cold
As she trudged through snow and sleet;
And her nose was long and cold
And her shoes were full of feet.

Harvey's favourite doctor doctor joke

'Doctor, doctor, I've just swallowed a sheep.'
'How do you feel?'
'Baa-aa-ad.'

Harvey's favourite waiter waiter joke

*'Waiter, waiter, is there rice pudding on the
menu?'*
'There was, sir, but I've wiped it off.'

Harvey's favourite daft definition

WAGGING TAIL – Something with a happy ending.

Harvey's favourite graffiti

*MY BROTHER GOT PUT INSIDE FOR FLAT
FEET*
His feet were in the wrong flat.

Harvey's favourite limerick

There was a young student of Crete
Who stood on his head in the street.
Said he, 'It is clear
If I mean to stop here
I shall have to shake hands with my feet.'

Harvey's favourite elephant joke

*What should you do when an elephant breaks a
    toe?*
Ring for a tow truck.

Harvey's favourite ghost joke

Where does a ghost train stop?
At a manifestation.

Harvey's favourite school joke

If you lost four fingers in an accident, what would you have?
No more piano lessons.

Harvey's favourite family joke

A man walked into a shop selling dress fabrics and said:
'I'd like three yards of satan for my wife.'
'You mean *satin,* sir,' said the assistant politely. '*Satan* is something that looks like the devil.'
'Oh, you've seen my wife, then?'

Harvey's favourite funny book title

Strong Winds by Gail Force

Harvey's favourite misprint

'The Ladies of the Helping Hand Society enjoyed a swap social evening on Friday. Everybody brought along something they no longer needed. Many of the women brought along their husbands.'

Arizona Star

Harvey's favourite pun joke

What name would you give to a bald koala?
Fred Bear.

Harvey's favourite riddle

Some ducks were walking down a path. There was a duck in front of two ducks, a duck behind two ducks, and a duck between two ducks. How many ducks in all?
Three ducks walking in a line.

Harvey's top favourite joke of all time

ICE SKATER: *Last year I broke my nose in six different places.*

FRIEND: That's impossible.

ICE SKATER: *No, it's not. I broke it in London, Newcastle, Manchester, Birmingham, Leeds and Edinburgh.*

Isadora's top twenty

Isadora's favourite shaggy dog story

A man called on a married couple whom he had not seen for several years. The door was opened by the wife.

'How lovely to see you again after all this time!' she exclaimed.

'It's nice to see you too,' said the man. 'And how is your husband Jack?'

'Of course, you don't know,' she said, 'Jack died last year.'

'I am so sorry,' said the man. 'Was it sudden?'

'Yes. One Sunday morning', she said, 'he went down the garden to pull a cabbage for lunch and dropped down dead.'

'How dreadful,' said the man. 'Whatever did you do?'

'What could I do?' rejoined the woman. 'I had to open a tin of peas.'

Isadora's favourite wisecrack

'What do you do when all the world is grey and gloomy?'
'I deliver the milk.'

Isadora's favourite knock knock

Knock, knock.
Who's there?
Isadora.
Isadora who?
Isadoran exit?

Isadora's favourite animal joke

Why is a skunk in the kitchen like a fire?
The sooner you put it out the better.

Isadora's favourite monster joke

1ST MONSTER: *That girl just rolled her eyes at me.*
2ND MONSTER: Roll them back again — she might
need them.

Isadora's favourite potty poem

Down the street his funeral goes
As sobs and wails diminish.
He died from drinking varnish,
But he had a lovely finish.

Isadora's favourite doctor doctor joke

'Doctor, doctor, I feel like a pack of cards.'
'Sit down. I'll deal with you later.'

Isadora's favourite waiter waiter joke

'Waiter, waiter, there's a film on my soup.'
'Is it a comedy or a thriller?'

Isadora's favourite daft definition

URCHIN — Lower part of a woman's face.

Isadora's favourite graffiti

CLEAN THE INSIDE OF YOUR WINDOWS, NOT THE OUTSIDE. YOU'LL BE ABLE TO SEE OUT BUT THE NEIGHBOURS WON'T SEE IN!

Isadora's favourite limerick

A girl who weighed many an oz
Used language I dare not pronoz,
When a fellow unkind
Pulled her chair out behind
Just to see, so he said, if she'd boz.

Isadora's favourite elephant joke

What do you call an elephant that flies?
A Jumbo Jet.

Isadora's favourite ghost joke

How do ghosts get through a locked door?
With a skeleton key.

Isadora's favourite school joke

TEACHER: *What do Zulus do with old banana skins?*
PUPIL: Throw them away, of course!

Isadora's favourite family joke

Two men met in the street for the first time in twenty years. The first man asked,
　'How's life been treating you?'
　'Not too good,' the friend answered. 'My wife left me, my son was arrested for stealing cars, my daughter is in hospital with a broken leg. On top of that, I'm going bald, I've got to have all my teeth out tomorrow, and my favourite dog just died.'
　'I'm sorry to hear that,' said the man. 'What line of business are you in?'
　'I sell lucky charms . . .'

Isadora's favourite funny book title

Solving the Mystery by Ivor Clue

Isadora's favourite misprint

'Recently Mrs Richardson invested in a cow, and she is now supplying the whole neighbourhood with milk, butter and eggs.'

Ely Standard

Isadora's favourite pun joke

Sign in a beauty parlour:

WE WORK SO HARD WE'LL EVEN DYE FOR YOU

Isadora's favourite riddle

Why did the science teacher take a ruler to bed?
To see how long he slept.

Isadora's top favourite joke of all time

What do you call a woman with a radiator on her head?
Anita.

James's top twenty

James's favourite shaggy dog story

A garage proprietor in Texas swore that the brand of petrol he sold was superior to all others, and especially to that of his rival across the road. One day, however, when he was having trouble with his Cadillac, the rival proprietor managed to persuade him to try *his* brand of petrol, and sure enough, the Cadillac engine roared into life. Its owner grinned wryly and said, 'You're right, your gas is as good as mine.'

James's favourite wisecrack

'I passed your house yesterday.'
'Thanks. I appreciate it.'

James's favourite knock knock

Knock, knock.
Who's there?
Ammonia.
Ammonia who?
Ammonia little person. I can't reach the bell.

James's favourite animal joke

What is the best way to get a wild duck?
Buy a tame one and irritate it!

James's favourite monster joke

What is a monster's final drink?
His bier.

James's favourite potty poem

Some say that fleas are black
But I know that is not so,
'Cos Mary had a little lamb
With fleas as white as snow.

James's favourite doctor doctor joke

'Doctor, doctor, I can't stop pulling ugly faces.'
'That's not a serious problem.'
'But people with ugly faces don't like it.'

James's favourite waiter waiter joke

'Waiter, waiter, how long will my sausages be?'
'About four inches.'

James's favourite daft definition

WALTZ – Something that belongs to Walter.

James's favourite graffiti

*HOW DOES A ONE-MAN BUS MOVE WHEN
THE DRIVER IS UPSTAIRS COLLECTING
THE FARES?*

James's favourite limerick

There was a young lady named Sue
Who carried a frog in each shoe.
When asked to stop
She replied with a hop,
'I'm trying to get into Who's Zoo!'

James's favourite elephant joke

What is yellow outside, grey on the inside, and has a wonderful memory?
An elephant omelette.

James's favourite ghost joke

What jewels do ghosts wear?
Tomb stones.

James's favourite funny book title

One Hundred Metres to the Bus Stop by Willy Makit, illustrated by Betty Wont

James's favourite school joke

Why did the teacher marry the caretaker?
Because he swept her off her feet!

James's favourite family joke

AUNTIE ELSIE: *My nextdoor neighbour is so old, she knew Madame Butterfly when she was still a cocoon.*

AUNTIE ENID: So what? There's a woman in my street who knew Eve when she was still a rib.

James's favourite misprint

'Blend sugar, flour and salt. Add egg and milk, cook until creamy in double boiler. Stir frequently. Add rest of ingredients. Mix well and serve chilled. Funeral service will be held Thursday afternoon at two o'clock.'

Reedsburg Post

James's favourite pun joke

What do you call a midget novelist?
A short story writer.

James's favourite riddle

How can you tell a pair of golf socks from an ordinary pair?
They usually have a hole in one.

James's favourite joke of all time

Two schoolchildren were walking to school one day.

'I don't think my parents like me,' said one boy.

'What makes you think that?' asked the other.

'Well, when my mother gives me my packed lunch for school she always wraps my sandwiches in a road map.'

Katy's top twenty

Katy's favourite shaggy dog story

A famous newspaper editor was once dining in a very smart French restaurant in Mayfair. As each course was served he sang its praises, and finally asked to see the chef so he could find out how he produced such delicious dishes. The chef was delighted by his praise, but shook his head sadly when the editor asked him for one of the recipes. 'I'm sorry, sir,' he said, 'but good chefs, like good journalists, never reveal their sauces.'

Katy's favourite wisecrack

'Does this train stop at Paddington?'
'If it doesn't there'll be a mighty big crash.'

Katy's favourite knock knock

Knock, knock.
Who's there?
Dishwasher.
Dishwasher who?
Dishwasher the way I spoke before I had false teeth.

Katy's favourite monster joke

Where do monsters go swimming?
The Dead Sea.

Katy's favourite animal joke

What do you give a pig with spots?
Oinkment.

Katy's favourite potty poem

Last night I slew my wife,
Stretched her on the parquet flooring;
I was loth to take her life,
But I had to stop her snoring.

Katy's favourite doctor doctor joke

*'Doctor, doctor, I have a terrible problem. Can you
help me out?'*
'Certainly. Which way did you come in?'

Katy's favourite waiter waiter joke

'Waiter, waiter, the service here is terrible.'
'If you think the service is terrible, wait until
 you see the food!'

Katy's favourite daft definition

NIGHTINGALE – A very windy evening.

Katy's favourite graffiti

*STAMP OUT VANDALISM OR I'LL BREAK
YOUR WINDOWS*

Katy's favourite limerick

Said an envious erudite ermine:
'There's one thing I cannot determine;
When a girl wears my coat
She's a person of note,
But when I do I'm only called vermin.'

Katy's favourite elephant joke

Two elephants fell off a cliff.
Boom! Boom!

Katy's favourite ghost joke

Where do ghosts get their jokes from?
A crypt writer.

Katy's favourite school joke

What is the most popular phrase at school?
I don't know!

Katy's favourite family joke

CECIL: *I was going to buy you a handkerchief for your birthday.*

AUNTIE DOROTHY: That was a very kind thought, Cecil. Why didn't you?

CECIL: *I couldn't find one big enough for your nose.*

Katy's favourite funny book title

Food on the Plate by E. Tittup

Katy's favourite misprint

'Mr Anthony Harris, playing solo trumpet in the Bedford Band, was awarded the medal for the best trombone player in the section.'

Sheffield Telegraph

Katy's favourite pun joke

A bus conductor was helping a very fat lady on to the bus.

'You want to take some yeast, Mother! It will help you rise better,' he joked.

'You take some yourself,' she retorted, 'then you'd be better bred.'

Katy's favourite riddle

What is an obtuse angle?
A thick ancient Briton.

Katy's top favourite joke of all time

SCOTTISH FATHER: *What would you like for Christmas?*

JIMMY: Well, I've got ma eye on a new bike.

SCOTTISH FATHER: *You keep your eye on it, 'cos you'll never get yer bum on it.*

Louis's top twenty

Louis's favourite shaggy dog story

An Englishman was playing cricket in a test match in Australia. He was facing an Australian fast bowler in a very tense match when a ball bounced and hit him straight in the eye. The next thing he knew, he was lying in a Melbourne hospital bed where he had had an emergency operation, and one side of his head was covered totally in bandages.

The surgeon who had performed the operation came to see how he was.

'Tell me, doctor,' said the man. 'What is the situation?'

'Well,' said the surgeon, 'I managed to save your eye.'

'That's wonderful,' said the cricketer.

'We'll give it to you when you leave as a souvenir,' said the surgeon.

Louis's favourite wisecrack

'That hat fits you nicely.'
'Yes, but what happens when my ears get tired?'

Louis's favourite knock knock

Knock, knock.
Who's there?
Tick.
Tick who?
Tick 'em up! I'm a tongue-tied towboy.

Louis's favourite animal joke

What did the grizzly take on holiday?
The bear essentials.

Louis's favourite monster joke

How do you get service in a monster guest house?
Just scream.

Louis's favourite potty poem

I shot an arrow in the air.
It fell to earth
I know not where.
I lose all my arrows that way!

Louis's favourite doctor doctor joke

'Doctor, doctor, I feel like a billiard ball.'
'Get to the back of the queue.'

Louis's favourite waiter waiter joke

'Waiter, waiter, there's a button in my salad.'
'It must have come off while the salad was dressing.'

Louis's favourite daft definition

PANTHER – Someone who makes panths.

Louis's favourite graffiti

I LIKE MAKING MUD PIES
(I hope you wash your hands before you eat them.)

Louis's favourite limerick

God's plan made a hopeful beginning
But man spoiled his chances by sinning.
We trust that God's glory
Will end up the story
But at present the other side's winning!

Louis's favourite elephant joke

What's the difference between an elephant and an apple?
Have you ever tried peeling an elephant?

Louis's favourite ghost joke

What do you find in a haunted cellar?
Whines and spirits.

Louis's favourite school joke

Did you hear about the abnormal student? He remembered to bring his homework back after the holidays.

Louis's favourite family joke

LOUIS: *My family are very, very rich.*
QUEENIE: How rich?
LOUIS: *Well, we've got three swimming pools.*
QUEENIE: Why three?
LOUIS: *One hot, one cold and one empty.*
QUEENIE: What's the empty one for?
LOUIS: *For people who can't swim.*

Louis's favourite funny book title

At The South Pole by Anne Tarctic

Louis's favourite misprint

'Said a Farnborough shopkeeper: "The Council are pulling the bread and butter out from under our feet."'

Hampshire paper

Louis's favourite pun joke

What is Britain's national flower?
The cost-of-living rose.

Louis's favourite riddle

Why do bulldogs have flat faces?
Through chasing parked cars.

Louis's top favourite joke of all time

A magician sauntered into a variety agent's office and announced that he had a new and totally original act.

'What can you do?' asked the agent.

'I saw a woman in half,' said the magician.

'That's one of the oldest tricks in the business,' exclaimed the agent. 'Every magician I know saws a lady in half.'

'Yes,' said the illusionist, 'but lengthways?'

Matilda's top twenty

Matilda's favourite shaggy dog story

A man went to a barber's shop and explained that he wanted a very special haircut because he was going on holiday to Italy for two weeks, during which time he hoped to visit the Vatican and meet the Pope. When he had finished, the barber said:

'I hope you enjoy your holiday. Do let me know all about it when you return.'

A few weeks later the same man returned to have his hair trimmed again.

'How did your trip to Italy go?' asked the barber.

'We had a marvellous time,' said the man. 'I visited the Vatican and was able to meet the Pope, and he even said a few words to me.'

'That was a great honour for you,' said the barber. 'What did the Pope say to you?'

The man replied: 'He shook my hand, stared at me, and said "Who the heck cut your hair like that?"'

Matilda's favourite wisecrack

'Why are you eating a banana with the skin on?'
'Oh, it's all right. I know what's inside.'

Matilda's favourite knock knock

Knock, knock.
Who's there?
Matilda.
Matilda who?
Matilda not to do it, but she would insist.

Matilda's favourite animal joke

Why do lions scratch themselves?
They're the only ones that know where they itch.

Matilda's favourite potty poem

Little Jack Horner sat in a corner
Eating his Christmas pie.
He put in his thumb, but instead of a plum
He squirted fruit juice in his eye.

Matilda's favourite monster joke

MOTHER MONSTER: Don't sit in that chair – it's for Rigor Mortis to set in.

Matilda's favourite doctor doctor joke

'Doctor, doctor, I keep thinking I'm a fly.'
'Just come down off the ceiling and let's talk about it.'

Matilda's favourite waiter waiter joke

'Waiter, waiter, do you have pig's trotters?'
'No, it's just that these new shoes are killing me.'

Matilda's favourite daft definition

REVOLVING DOOR – Place to go around with people.

Matilda's favourite graffiti

WHY DON'T THEY HAVE A RADIO PHONE-IN FOR THE DEAF?

Matilda's favourite limerick

There was an old man of Vancouver
Whose wife got sucked into the hoover.
He said, 'There's some doubt
If she's more in than out
But whichever it is, I can't move her.'

Matilda's favourite elephant joke

'What's the difference between an elephant and a pint of milk?'
'I don't know.'
'Well, I'm not sending you out for a pint of milk!'

Matilda's favourite ghost joke

FIRST GHOST: *I don't seem to frighten anyone these days.*

SECOND GHOST: No, we might just as well be dead for all they care.

Matilda's favourite school joke

Why did the schoolboy stand on his head?
He was turning things over in his mind.

Matilda's favourite family joke

GRANDPA: *That steak you gave me last night was terrible. I hope you've given me something tonight I can get my teeth into.*

GRANDMA: Yes, I have – here's a glass of water.

Matilda's favourite funny book title

The Calypso Band by Lydia Dustbin

Matilda's favourite misprint

'Mr Bromsgrove suffered a stroke on 24 July 1984 but with the loving care of his family, and the kind attention of his nurse, he never fully recovered.'

Crewe Chronicle

Matilda's favourite pun joke

SHOPPER IN CANNIBAL SUPERMARKET: How's your husband these days?

FRIEND: Moaning about his health as usual. To hear him talk you'd think he'd got one foot in the gravy!

Matilda's favourite riddle

How do you make gold soup?
Start with fourteen carrots.

Matilda's top favourite joke of all time

Two men were riding on a train for the first time. They had taken a bunch of bananas to eat on the journey. Just as the train approached a tunnel the first man took a bite of his banana.

'Have you tasted your banana yet?' he asked his friend.

'No,' replied the friend.

'Well, for goodness' sake don't! I took one bite and went blind!'

Nigel's top twenty

Nigel's favourite shaggy dog story

During the winter's very violent snowstorms, a village in the mountains became totally cut off from the rest of the world. A Red Cross team was carried by helicopter to within a mile of the village, all but covered in snow.

The rescuers struggled through deep drifts, by foot and by shovelling their way through. Eventually they reached the first house in the village, and they shovelled away enough snow to reach the door. Finally the door was opened, and one of the rescuers stepped forward and said:

'We're from the Red Cross.'

'Well,' said the inhabitant, 'it's been a very tough winter and I don't think we can give you anything for your collection this year.'

Nigel's favourite wisecrack

'Do you think I'll lose my looks as I get older?'
'If you're lucky!'

Nigel's favourite knock knock

Knock, knock.
Who's there?
Ivor.
Ivor who?
Ivor you let me in or I climb through the window.

Nigel's favourite animal joke

*'I want you to keep that dog out of the house. It's
    full of fleas.'*
'Fido! Don't go in that house. It's full of fleas!'

Nigel's favourite monster joke

How do monster snowmen feel when they melt?
Abominable.

Nigel's favourite limerick

There was a young lady named Hannah
Who slipped on a peel of banana.
She wanted to swear
But her mother was there
So she whistled 'The Star-spangled Banner'.

Nigel's favourite potty poem

Here I sit in the moonlight,
Abandoned by women and men,
Muttering over and over,
'I'll never eat garlic again!'

Nigel's favourite doctor doctor joke

'Doctor, doctor, I have trouble getting to sleep at nights.'
'Lie right on the edge of the bed – you'll soon drop off.'

Nigel's favourite waiter waiter joke

'Waiter, waiter, this lemonade is all cloudy!'
'Don't worry, sir, it's the glass that's dirty.'

Nigel's favourite daft definition

PEEPHOLE – A group of human beings.

Nigel's favourite graffiti

I'VE INVENTED A NEW INSECTICIDE – IT KILLS THE CROPS SO THAT THE INSECTS STARVE TO DEATH

Nigel's favourite elephant joke

PATIENT: *Doctor, I keep seeing elephants with big green spots.*
DOCTOR: Have you ever seen a psychiatrist?
PATIENT: *No, just elephants with big green spots.*

Nigel's favourite ghost joke

What do you get if you cross a ghost with a packet of crisps?
Snacks that go crunch in the night.

Nigel's favourite school joke

TEACHER: *How can you prove that the world is round?*

PUPIL: I never said it was, miss.

Nigel's favourite family joke

A husband and wife had been fighting for a long time. Life seemed to be one long battle. One afternoon the husband was walking home from work when he was knocked down by a hit-and-run driver. As he lay in the gutter a policeman rushed up to him.

'Did you see who it was?' asked the policeman.

'No, I didn't actually see,' said the man, 'but I know it was my wife.'

'How do you know if it was your wife if you couldn't see who was driving?'

'I'd recognize that laugh anywhere.'

Nigel's favourite funny book title

Never Give Up by Percy Vere

Nigel's favourite misprint

'If you bought our manual "How to fly solo in ten easy lessons" we apologize for the fact that we did not include the final chapter "How to land your plane". Just send us your name and address and we will send it to you at once.'

Eastmid News Service

Nigel's favourite pun joke

'Did you like the new restaurant?'

'It wasn't a restaurant – it was more like a Bureau of Missing Portions.'

Nigel's favourite riddle

What is the cheapest way to hire a horse?
Put four bricks under its feet.

Nigel's top favourite joke of all time

A doctor was examining a sick boy in his surgery. Suddenly he came into the waiting room and asked the receptionist for a screwdriver. She gave him one and he returned to his surgery. A few minutes later he came out and asked for a hammer and chisel.

'For goodness' sake!' cried the anxious mother. 'What's the matter with my little boy?'

'I don't know yet,' said the doctor. 'I can't get my medicine bag open.'

Olive's top twenty

Olive's favourite shaggy dog story

An Englishman was in a Scottish restaurant, when suddenly he sneezed so violently that his false teeth flew out of his mouth and shot straight across the room, where they smashed against a wall.

'Don't worry,' said the waiter, 'my brother will get you a new set of teeth much cheaper than an English dentist will charge, and he can provide them almost immediately.'

'That's marvellous,' said the Englishman. 'I didn't know what I was going to do without my teeth.'

He couldn't believe his luck when the waiter returned after less than five minutes with another set of teeth. The Englishman tried them and they fitted perfectly.

'I can't thank you enough,' said the Englishman. 'Your brother must be a very clever dentist.'

'Oh, he's not a dentist,' replied the waiter. 'He's an undertaker.'

Olive's favourite wisecrack

'I choose my own clothes.'
'It seems to be moth that chews mine.'

Olive's favourite knock knock

Knock, knock.
Who's there?
Olive.
Olive who?
Olive here. What's your excuse?

Olive's favourite animal joke

Why are pelicans expensive to feed?
They present very large bills.

Olive's favourite monster joke

Why are vampires crazy?
They're often bats.

Olive's favourite potty poem

I was playing golf the day
   That Germans landed;
All our troops had run away,
   All our ships were stranded;
And the thought of England's shame
   Altogether spoilt my game.

Olive's favourite doctor doctor joke

*'Doctor, doctor, will my measles be better next
   week?'*
'I never make rash promises.'

Olive's favourite waiter waiter joke

*'Waiter, waiter, what does this fly in the bottom of
   my cup mean?'*
'I'm a waiter, madam, not a fortune teller.'

Olive's favourite daft definition

ALLOCATE – Way of greeting a girl named
Catherine.

Olive's favourite graffiti

COMMIT SUICIDE THE IRISH WAY
Slip arsenic in your tea while looking the other
way.

Olive's favourite limerick

A traveller once, to his sorrow
Requested a ticket to Morrow.
Said the agent, 'It's plain
That there isn't a train
To Morrow today, but tomorrow!'

Olive's favourite elephant joke

What do you give a seasick elephant?
Plenty of room!

Olive's favourite ghost joke

Which airline do ghosts use?
British Scareways.

Olive's favourite school joke

What happened to the plant in the maths class?
It grew square roots.

Olive's favourite family joke

OLIVE: *My grandmother fell down some steps last night.*
FRANCIS: Cellar?
OLIVE: *No, I think she can be repaired.*

Olive's favourite funny book title

Who Killed Cock Robin? by Howard I. Know

Olive's favourite misprint

'The service was held at 11.00 a.m. by the Rev. John Hamill whose theme was "Evil Member in the Church". The choir sang the anthem "Who Can It Be?"'

Columbus Dispatch

Olive's favourite pun joke

Remember, it's better to have loved a short person than never to have loved a tall.

Olive's favourite riddle

Why don't astronauts keep their jobs very long?
Because as soon as they start they get fired.

Olive's top favourite joke of all time

Grandad went into the Post Office to collect his pension. He hadn't got a pen with him, so he signed for it in pencil. This was not acceptable, so the man behind the counter said:

'Would you mind inking it over, sir?'

Grandad went away and came back five minutes later.

'I've thought it over,' he said, 'and I still want my pension.'

Paul's top twenty

Paul's favourite shaggy dog story

Dimitri Bulganivitch, the Soviet Union's top secret agent, arrived in Swansea, Wales, on a highly secret mission. His superiors in Moscow had told Bulganivitch to make contact with a man called Jones, and so he made his way at once to the address he had been given. He eventually reached the building, which was a block of flats, and was taken aback when he saw that eight people in the building all had the name Jones.

Risking everything, the ruthless secret agent decided to take a chance and knock at the door of the first Jones in the building. As the door was opened, Bulganivitch whispered the secret message he had been given in code:

'Cabbages are pretty and little lambs eat ivy.'

'Sorry,' came the reply, 'I'm Jones the Milk. You'll be wanting Jones the Spy – two floors up.'

Paul's favourite wisecrack

'How can I get to the hospital fast?'
'Just stand in the middle of the road.'

Paul's favourite knock knock

Knock, knock.
Who's there?
Paul.
Paul who?
Paul harder and maybe the door will open.

Paul's favourite animal joke

What do you get if you cross a skunk with a boomerang?
A nasty smell you can't get rid of.

Paul's favourite monster joke

Why did the monster stop playing with his brother?
He got tired of kicking him around.

Paul's favourite doctor doctor joke

'Doctor, doctor, I'm having terrible trouble with these contact lenses. I just can't get them over my glasses.'

Paul's favourite waiter waiter joke

'Waiter, waiter, this soup's disgusting.'
'No, it's oxtail, sir.'

Paul's favourite daft definition

HALFWIT – Someone who is funny half of the time.

Paul's favourite graffiti

I'M AN IRISH TINKER
Oh, and what are you tinking about?

Paul's favourite potty poem

Sweet little Eileen Rose
Was tired and sought some sweet repose.
But her naughty sister Clare
Placed a pin upon her chair
And sweet little Eileen rose!

Paul's favourite elephant joke

*How can you tell if there's an elephant in your
    oven?*
You can't shut the door.

Paul's favourite ghost joke

What is the best way to describe horror films?
Spooktacular.

Paul's favourite limerick

When accepting a young man at Kew,
A maiden said, 'Yes, I'll be true.
But you must understand,
As you've asked for my hand,
That the rest of me goes with it too!'

Paul's favourite school joke

TEACHER: *Why did the Romans build straight roads?*
PUPIL: So the Britons couldn't hide round corners.

Paul's favourite family joke

The recently widowed Mrs Brown went to a seance and asked the medium if she could get in touch with her late husband.

'Yes, certainly,' said the medium.

'Oh, thank goodness for that!' exclaimed Mrs Brown.

'Why is it so urgent? asked the medium.

'I've just locked myself out of the house,' said Mrs Brown, 'and he's the only one that knows where the spare key is hidden.'

Paul's favourite funny book title

Grow Your Own Vegetables by Rosa Carrots

Paul's favourite misprint

'The Council is cutting down on unnecessary postage costs by asking householders to collect their rates bill. They will be writing to every householder to inform them of this fact.'

Bristol Evening News

Paul's favourite pun joke

PAUL: *What does t-e-r-r-i-f-y spell?*
CAROL: Terrify.
PAUL: *And what does t-i-s-s-u-e spell?*
CAROL: Tissue.
PAUL: *Put them both together.*
CAROL: Terrify tissue?
PAUL: *Not at all – carry on!*

Paul's favourite riddle

How did Noah manage in the dark?
He used ark-lights or flood-lights.

Paul's top favourite joke of all time

CUSTOMER: *Is it all right to boil-wash this cardigan?*
SHOP ASSISTANT: Yes, as long as you boil it in warm water.

Queenie's top twenty

Queenie's favourite shaggy dog story

A man was driving through the dead of night when suddenly his car broke down. It was too late to find a garage and he seemed to be miles from the nearest telephone box. As it was a cold night and he did not feel like staying in the car, he walked off in the hope of finding a cottage or farmhouse where he could spend the night.

Presently he came across a monastery. There was a candle burning in the window, so he knocked at the door and a monk let him in and agreed to let him stay the night. He was put into a small cell which contained a very uncomfortable bed, but it was better than sleeping in the car. In the room was a large box, and he asked the monk what was inside.

'I can't possibly tell you,' he said. 'You have to be a monk to find out.'

During the night strange noises started coming from the box, and the man was very tempted to look inside but knew that something dreadful would happen to him if he did. All night he lay awake thinking about the contents of the box.

In the morning he knew that he just had to find out, and so he enrolled as a monk. For several long years he trained as a monk and eventually was taken back to the monastery and into the little cell where the box still stood. He lifted the lid off the box and looked inside. Inside the box he saw . . . sorry, I can't tell you. You have to be a monk to find out!

Queenie's favourite wisecrack

'I hear you bought a diamond ring for £1.50?'
'Yes. It didn't have a stone in it, though.'

Queenie's favourite knock knock

Knock, knock.
Who's there?
Queenie.
Queenie who?
Queenie's gwasses for me, pwease.

Queenie's favourite animal joke

'Did you put the cat out?'
'No, was it on fire again?'

Queenie's favourite monster joke

What do you call an Egyptian Pharaoh that eats biscuits in its tomb?
A crummy mummy.

Queenie's favourite potty poem

A dog is loved
By old and young.
He wags his tail
And not his tongue.

Queenie's favourite doctor doctor joke

'Doctor, doctor, I can't stop telling lies.'
'You don't expect me to believe that, do you?'

Queenie's favourite waiter waiter joke

*'Waiter, waiter, there's no rabbit in this rabbit
    pie.'*
'Well, you don't get any dog in dog biscuits, do
    you?'

Queenie's favourite daft definition

RHUBARB – Embarrassed celery.

Queenie's favourite graffiti

MY FATHER MENDED SIXTEEN BROKEN WINDOWS IN OUR HOUSE, THEN HE DISCOVERED HIS GLASSES WERE CRACKED

Queenie's favourite limerick

There once was a phantom named Pete
Who never would play, drink or eat.
He said, 'I don't care
For a Coke or éclair,
Can't you see that I'm dead on my feet?'

Queenie's favourite elephant joke

'I can lift an elephant with one hand.'
'Yes, but where would you find a one-handed elephant?'

Queenie's favourite ghost joke

Did you hear about the Irish ghost? It climbed over a wall.

Queenie's favourite school joke

TEACHER: *Who wrote 'To a Field Mouse'?*
PUPIL: Whoever it was, I bet he didn't get a reply.

Queenie's favourite family joke

FATHER: *I just can't understand why you don't get good marks in arithmetic at school. It was my best subject.*
QUEENIE: But Dad, I did get 9 out of 10.
FATHER: *Yes, but 60 per cent isn't good enough.*

Queenie's favourite funny book title

The Post-Script by Adeline Extra

Queenie's favourite misprint

'Colonel Morooney, the bottle-scarred veteran, died at his home last week aged 92.'

Wiltshire paper

Queenie's favourite pun joke

What does the British government use when it takes a census of monkeys in the zoo?
An ape recorder.

Queenie's favourite riddle

How do you keep a skunk from smelling?
Hold its nose.

Queenie's top favourite joke of all time

DANCER: *Will you play* 'We'll Gather Lilacs'?
BANDLEADER: But that's the tune we just played.
DANCER: *I wish I'd known – it's my favourite.*

Roger's top twenty

Roger's favourite shaggy dog story

A man went into a restaurant with his dog. He sat down at the table, and his dog sat on the chair opposite. It was not long before the waitress appeared.

'I'm sorry, sir,' she said, 'but we cannot allow dogs in this restaurant.'

'But this is no ordinary dog,' said the man. 'This is a talking dog.'

'It makes no difference if he can juggle the cutlery – we don't allow dogs in this restaurant.'

The man refused to leave, so the waitress went off and returned with the manager.

'I'm sorry, sir,' said the manager, 'but I do not allow dogs in my restaurant.'

'But this is a talking dog,' said the man. 'Not just an ordinary mongrel.'

'OK,' said the manager, 'if the dog can talk, you can both stay. Right – what is above this restaurant?'

'R-r-r-oof,' said the dog.

'There, I knew he couldn't talk!' said the manager. 'Now both of you get out!'

When they got outside, the dog looked up at its master and said:

'Oh, look! Above the restaurant is a beauty parlour!'

Roger's favourite wisecrack

'My little sister just fell down a hole. What shall I do?'
'Dash to the library and get a book on raising children.'

Roger's favourite knock knock

Knock, knock.
Who's there?
Luke.
Luke who?
Luke through the keyhole and you'll see.

Roger's favourite animal joke

Who took Little Bo Peep's sheep?
The crook she had with her.

Roger's favourite monster joke

Did you hear about the girl monster who wasn't pretty and wasn't ugly? She was pretty ugly.

Roger's favourite potty poem

'Twas in a restaurant they met,
Romeo and Juliet.
He had no cash to pay the debt
So Romeo'd what Juliet.

Roger's favourite doctor doctor joke

'Doctor, doctor, I think I'm a bird.'
'Just perch yourself down and I'll tweet you in a minute.'

Roger's favourite waiter waiter joke

'Waiter, waiter, this egg is horrible.'
'Don't blame me – I only laid the table.'

Roger's favourite daft definition

UNIT – A term of abuse.

Roger's favourite graffiti

MY SISTER'S A MANIOKLEPTIC
She walks backwards into shops and leaves things.

Roger's favourite elephant joke

Why shouldn't you go into the jungle after six o'clock?
Because of elephants falling out of trees.

Roger's favourite limerick

A farmer once called his cow 'Zephyr'
She seemed such a breezy young heifer.
When the farmer drew near
She kicked off his ear
And now the old farmer's much deafer.

Roger's favourite ghost joke

Where do ghosts like to have parties?
The morgue the merrier.

Roger's favourite school joke

MOTHER: I won't say my son's hopeless at school,
  but he has to cheat to come last.

Roger's favourite family joke

BROTHER: *How come you're so clever?*
SISTER: I take clever pills.
BROTHER: *Let me have some, then.*
SISTER: Take two of these.
BROTHER: *These aren't pills – they're just sweets.*
SISTER: See! They're starting to work already.

Roger's favourite funny book title

The Ugly Hag by Ida Face

Roger's favourite misprint

'It is small wonder that morale is low. Dentists badly paid for their work are pulling out in droves.'

The Practitioner

Roger's favourite pun joke

What did the meat say when it was about to be put on a skewer?

'Oh, spear me! Spear me!'

Roger's favourite riddle

Why is a rabbit's nose shiny?

Because its powder puff is at the wrong end.

Roger's top favourite joke of all time

GUEST: *Didn't you say this guest house was only a stone's throw from the sea?*

LANDLADY: Keep practising – you'll soon be able to throw it two miles.

Sally's top twenty

Sally's favourite shaggy dog story

A teddy bear was looking for work and eventually got himself a job on a building site. His first task was to lay the foundations for a house, and he was given a pickaxe by the foreman so that he could break up some rocks and old concrete.

The teddy bear was quite happy doing this and enjoyed swinging his pickaxe through the air. He got so carried away that before he knew where he was a bell was ringing and it was time for lunch. He laid down his pickaxe and off he went for something to eat.

When he returned, to his horror he discovered that his pickaxe was not lying where he had left it. Someone had obviously been along while he was at lunch and stolen it. Feeling very distressed he went along to the foreman and said:

'While I was at lunch someone came and stole my pickaxe.'

'It's your own fault,' said the foreman. 'Surely you know that today's the day the teddy bears have their pick nicked?'

Sally's favourite wisecrack

'I once ate a clock.'
'Wasn't that time consuming?'

Sally's favourite knock knock

Knock, knock.
Who's there?
Sally.
Sally who?
Salleluyah, at last you've answered the door!

Sally's favourite animal joke

*What did the horse say when it reached the end of
    its nosebag?*
'This is the last straw!'

Sally's favourite monster joke

Why are vampire families so close?
Because blood is thicker than water.

Sally's favourite potty poem

Jack and Jill went up the hill
To fetch a pail of water.
Jack fell down and broke his crown,
And sued the farmer and his daughter.

Sally's favourite doctor doctor joke

'Doctor, doctor, everyone keeps ignoring me.'
'Next patient, please!'

Sally's favourite waiter waiter joke

*'Waiter, waiter, I want a glass of milk and a piece
    of fish.'*
'Fillet?'
'Yes, right to the top of the glass, please.'

Sally's favourite daft definition

WASHABLE – A bull you can put in the spin dryer.

Sally's favourite graffiti

THE KIDS IN MY CLASS ARE SO TOUGH
THAT THE TEACHERS PLAY TRUANT

Sally's favourite limerick

There was an old man in a hearse
Who murmured, 'This might have been worse;
Of course the expense
Is simply immense,
But it doesn't come out of my purse!'

Sally's favourite elephant joke

Why did the elephant tie a knot in his trunk?
So that he wouldn't forget.

Sally's favourite ghost joke

Where do ghosts go on holiday?
Goole.

Sally's favourite school joke

TEACHER: *Have you read 'Freckles'?*
SALLY: No, I've got the brown kind.

Sally's favourite family joke

A man was playing the piano very loudly one
evening when suddenly there was a knock on the
door. It was the next-door neighbour.

'Do you know my wife's ill in bed next door?' he
asked.

'No,' said the man, 'but if you hum the tune I'm
sure I can pick it up.'

Sally's favourite funny book title

Army Jokes by Major Laugh

Sally's favourite misprint

'Never throw away old chicken bones, or those left from a roast. Put them in a pan of water and boil them for several hours with a few diced vegetables. It will make very delicious soap.'

New Zealand Woman's Weekly

Sally's favourite pun joke

'My sister plays a game every time she tries to sing.'
'What game is that?'
'Maim that tune.'

Sally's favourite riddle

What do you call a very tall Irishman?
Paddy Long Legs.

Sally's top favourite joke of all time

A young girl visited a fortune teller. The clairvoyant looked into her crystal ball and started laughing. Suddenly the girl slapped the woman right across the face.

'Why did you do that?' asked the fortune teller.

'Well,' said the girl, 'my mother told me I should always strike a happy medium.'

Thomas's top twenty

Thomas's favourite shaggy dog story

One day a man was walking down the road pulling a cabbage behind him on a lead. A lot of people looked at the man very strangely, but nobody said anything. Before long a policeman passed the man, and noticed that on the lead was a cabbage.

'The man must be a little strange,' thought the policeman, 'but I suppose I had better play along with him.'

So he went up to the man, bent down and patted the cabbage, and said:

'That's a nice little dog you've got there. What's its name?'

'That's not a dog,' said the man, looking at the policeman as if he were mad. 'It's a cabbage.'

'Oh,' said the policeman, looking puzzled. 'I thought you were just a little strange.'

The policeman walked off, scratching his head.

The man then looked down at the cabbage and said:

'That fooled him, didn't it, Rover?'

Thomas's favourite wisecrack

'While I was fishing I spotted a shark.
'Don't be silly – whoever heard of a spotted shark?'

Thomas's favourite knock knock

Knock, knock.
Who's there?
Alex.
Alex who?
Alexplain later.

Thomas's favourite animal joke

When is a baby giraffe even taller than its mother?
When it sits on its father's shoulders.

Thomas's favourite monster joke

How did Frankenstein's monster eat its food?
By bolting it down.

Thomas's favourite potty poem

If a man who 'turnips!' cries
Cries not when his father dies,
Is it not proof he'd rather
Have a turnip than his father?

Thomas's favourite doctor doctor joke

'Doctor, doctor, I feel so nervous. This is the first operation I've ever had.'
'Don't worry – this is the first operation I've ever performed.'

Thomas's favourite waiter waiter joke

'Waiter, waiter, your tie is in my soup.'
'Don't worry, sir, it won't shrink.'

Thomas's favourite daft definition

DECEIT – Piece of furniture with four legs that you sit on.

Thomas's favourite graffiti

WHY PAY TO VISIT A PSYCHIATRIST WHEN YOU CAN STAY AT HOME AND TALK TO THE CEILING FOR NOTHING?

Thomas's favourite limerick

The reason she smiled (Mona Lisa)
Was seeing the Tower of Pisa.
They didn't quite mean
To make the thing lean,
But they built it that way just to please 'er.

Thomas's favourite elephant joke

Why did the elephant paint her head yellow?
To see if blondes had more fun.

Thomas's favourite ghost joke

Which ghost was once president of France?
Charles De Ghoul.

Thomas's favourite school joke

TEACHER: *Do you know the capital of Alaska?*
PUPIL: Juneau?
TEACHER: *Yes, of course, but I'm asking you.*

Thomas's favourite family joke

MOTHER: *I think grandma needs new glasses.*
FATHER: Why do you say that?
MOTHER: *She's sitting in the kitchen watching the washing machine.*
FATHER: What's wrong with that?
MOTHER: *She's watching grandad's long johns going round and thinks she's watching the wrestling on television.*

Thomas's favourite funny book title

All You Need To Know About Explosives by Dinah Mite

Thomas's favourite misprint

'A set of traffic lights has been stolen from a main road junction in Exeter. A police spokesman said: "Some thieves will stop at nothing."'

Exeter Express & Echo

Thomas's favourite pun joke

What did the duck say to the waiter?
Why have you put this lunch on my bill?

Thomas's favourite riddle

What do you do when your nose goes on strike?
Picket.

Thomas's top favourite joke of all time

PATIENT: *I've been feeling very run down lately and I've been taking these vitamin pills, but they don't seem to be doing me any good.*

DOCTOR: It could have something to do with your diet. What have you been eating?

PATIENT: *You mean you have to eat as well as taking vitamin pills?*

Una's top twenty

Una's favourite shaggy dog story

Three boys went into a sweetshop.

'I want twenty-five pence worth of toffee,' said the first boy, 'the one that's on the top shelf.'

The shopkeeper went to the back of his shop, found his ladder, placed it under the shelf where the toffee was, climbed up and got twenty-five pence worth of toffee. He came down from the ladder and put it back into the back of the shop.

'That's twenty-five pence, please.'

He took the boy's money and then asked the second boy what he would like.

'I want twenty-five pence worth of toffee, please.'

The shopkeeper went into the back of his shop, brought out the ladder, climbed to the top shelf and got out the toffee. While still at the top of the ladder he looked down at the third boy and said:

'Do you want twenty-five pence worth of toffee too?'

'No,' replied the boy.

So the shopkeeper came down the ladder and put it carefully away in the back of the shop. He took the second boy's money, and then said to the third boy:

'And what would you like?'

'Thirty pence worth of toffee, please.'

Una's favourite wisecrack

'There's something wrong with my ear. Every time I put my finger in it, I can't hear!'

Una's favourite knock knock

Knock, knock.
Who's there?
Una.
Una who?
Una who I mean?

Una's favourite animal joke

How do you know if you've had a cat burglar?
It steals a saucer and a pint of milk.

Una's favourite monster joke

Which animal could go in a washing machine?
A wash-and-were-wolf.

Una's favourite potty poem

Humpty Dumpty sat on a wall,
Humpty Dumpty had a great fall.
All the King's horses and all the King's men
Cried, 'Oh, no! Scrambled eggs for breakfast
   again!'

Una's favourite doctor doctor joke

'Doctor, doctor, I've got a terribly sore throat.'
'Just go over to the window and stick your
   tongue out.'
'Will that cure it?'
No, I just don't like the woman who lives
   opposite.'

Una's favourite waiter waiter joke

'Waiter, waiter, what is this soup?'
'It's bean soup, sir.'
'I don't care what it's been. What is it now?'

Una's favourite daft definition

EGGWHITE – Snow White's brother.

Una's favourite graffiti

*NOTHING IS IMPOSSIBLE – I'VE BEEN
DOING NOTHING FOR YEARS*

Una's favourite limerick

There was a young fellow of Ceuta
Who rode into church on his scooter;
He knocked down the Dean
And said, 'Sorry, old bean,
I ought to have sounded my hooter.'

Una's favourite elephant joke

How do you get an elephant in a box of matches?
Take the matches out first.

Una's favourite ghost joke

What kind of horse does a headless horseman ride?
A nightmare.

Una's favourite school joke

FATHER: *Son, I want you to have something that I never had when I was at school.*
SON: What's that? Good marks?

Una's favourite family joke

HUSBAND: *I want you to bury my wife.*
UNDERTAKER: But I buried your wife last year.
HUSBAND: *Yes, but I remarried.*
UNDERTAKER: Oh, congratulations, sir.

Una's favourite funny book title

Who Saw Him Leave? by Wendy Go

Una's favourite misprint

'The new bride is approximately eighteen feet wide from buttress to buttress.'

Essex County Standard

Una's favourite pun joke

*What did the artist, Whistler, say when he found
 his mother wasn't sitting in her rocking chair?*
'Mum, you're off your rocker!'

Una's favourite riddle

What has the shortest life span?
New Year resolutions. They are born before
 midnight and dead and forgotten the next day.

Una's favourite joke of all time

'Do you know how to tell the age of a telephone?'
'No – how?'
'Count its rings.'

Victor's top twenty

Victor's favourite shaggy dog story

A gold mine in Alaska was in danger of being flooded in the spring thaw, and none of the miners were small enough to crawl through a narrow tunnel and close the tight-fitting gate that would have shut out the water. They were in despair when Shorty Jones, an exceptionally small and slimly built young man, turned up at the site and offered to go through the tunnel for them. 'It's a case,' he said, 'of a titch in time saving the mine.'

Victor's favourite knock knock

Knock, knock.
Who's there?
Victor.
Victor who?
Victor his trousers getting out of a tree.

Victor's favourite animal joke

What do you get if you cross a woodpecker with a parrot?
A bird that knocks on doors and delivers messages.

Victor's favourite wisecrack

'It says in this book that Eskimos eat whale meat and blubber.'
'I think I'd blubber if I had to eat whale meat all the time.'

Victor's favourite monster joke

Why did the monster buy two tickets to the zoo?
One to get in and one to get out.

Victor's favourite potty poem

The baker's wife, Matilda Jones,
Had loads and loads of fun,
For every time she did her hair
She put it in a bun.

Victor's favourite doctor doctor joke

'*Doctor, doctor, you think I'm overweight, don't you?*'
'Whatever makes you think that?'
'*The point during my check-up when you said, "Open your mouth and say Moooo . . ."*'

Victor's favourite waiter waiter joke

'*Waiter, waiter, how long have you worked here?*'
'Only two weeks, sir.'
'*Then it can't be you that took my order.*'

Victor's favourite daft definition

BLACKMAIL – A letter that the postman has dropped in the mud.

Victor's favourite graffiti

I DON'T LIKE MY AUNTIE BRIDGET – AM I ANTI-AUNTIE?

Victor's favourite limerick

There was an old man from Peru
Who dreamt he was eating his shoe.
He awoke in the night
In a terrible fright
And found it was perfectly true.

Victor's favourite elephant joke

What is the difference between an elephant and a biscuit?
You can't dip an elephant in your tea.

Victor's favourite ghost joke

What does a ghost give his wife for Christmas?
A girdle so that she can keep her ghoulish figure.

Victor's favourite school joke

'Did the music teacher say your voice was heavenly?'
'Not exactly – she said it was like nothing on earth.'

Victor's favourite family joke

HUSBAND: *Am I dying, Nellie?*
WIFE: Yes, you are, Walter.
HUSBAND: *Can I have one last request?*
WIFE: Of course you can. What is it?
HUSBAND: *Can I have a slice of your sponge cake over there?*
WIFE: No, you can't! I'm saving that for the funeral.

Victor's favourite funny book title

Dancing at the Party by
Hans Neesanboompsadaisy

Victor's favourite misprint

'Before Miss Pollard concluded the concert with her rendition of "At The End of a Perfect Day" she was prevented with a large bouquet of carnations from the mayoress.'

Staffordshire Evening Standard

Victor's favourite pun joke

A man had broken his false teeth and went to
buy some more. He was standing outside a shop
window choosing his new dentures when a
policeman came up and arrested him. He was
told that it was against the law to pick your teeth
in public.

Victor's favourite riddle

*Why wouldn't the idiot throw away his broken
clock?*
Because he said it was right twice a day.

Victor's top favourite joke of all time

A man walked into a bar and saw a baboon standing by the bar.

'A whisky with two slices of lemon, please,' said the baboon.

The barman poured out the drink, put in two slices of lemon and gave it to the baboon, who paid for it and sat down.

'Now there's something you don't often see,' said the man.

'You certainly don't,' said the barman. 'Most people have one slice of lemon.'

Wincy's top twenty

Wincy's favourite shaggy dog story

A very famous concert pianist used to practise the piano for an hour every morning. He gave his butler orders that under no circumstance whatsoever was he to be disturbed.

One morning someone arrived at the door and insisted upon seeing the pianist.

'I am sorry, sir,' said the butler, 'but I am afraid he is out.'

'He's not out!' insisted the visitor, 'why, as I came up the drive just now I heard him playing the piano.'

'I am sorry, sir,' said the butler, 'but I'm afraid you are mistaken. I was simply dusting the piano keys.'

Wincy's favourite wisecrack

'Did you go to Matilda's party?'
'No, the invitation said from four to eight, and I'm nine.'

Wincy's favourite knock knock

Knock, knock.
Who's there?
William.
William who?
Williamind your own business!

Wincy's favourite animal joke

What is the hardest part of milking a mouse?
Getting a bucket under it.

Wincy's favourite monster joke

Which monster has no luck?
The luckless monster.

Wincy's favourite potty poem

Don't worry if your life's a joke
And your successes few.
Remember that the mighty oak
Was once a nut like you!

Wincy's favourite doctor doctor joke

'Doctor, doctor, I feel like an apple.'
'Well, come over here. I won't bite you.'

Wincy's favourite waiter waiter joke

'Waiter, waiter, this coffee's weak.'
'What do you expect me to do – give it weight
training?'

Wincy's favourite daft definition

REBATE – Putting another worm on the hook.

Wincy's favourite graffiti

*EARN CASH IN YOUR SPARE TIME –
BLACKMAIL YOUR FRIENDS*

Wincy's favourite limerick

There was a young man of Devizes
Whose ears were of different sizes;
The one that was small
Was no use at all,
But the other won several prizes.

Wincy's favourite elephant joke

What do you give an exhausted elephant?
Trunkquillizers.

Wincy's favourite ghost joke

Why didn't the skeleton want to go to school?
Because his heart wasn't in it.

Wincy's favourite school joke

TEACHER: *Your writing seems to get worse instead of better.*
PUPIL: But if you could read my writing you'd notice my bad spelling.

Wincy's favourite family joke

BROTHER: *I have problems getting to sleep at night.*
SISTER: Why don't you count sheep?
BROTHER: *I tried. It doesn't work.*
SISTER: Why not?
BROTHER: *I can only count up to six.*

Wincy's favourite funny book title

Is It Love? by Midas Wellbe

Wincy's favourite misprint

'The Women's Institute will hold their fortnightly lecture in St Mary's Hall. The topic will be "Country Life" and Mrs Wills will show some slides of beautiful wild pants.'

Matlock Mercury

Wincy's favourite pun joke

WINCY: *Why are you going to become a baker?*
BOY: Because I need the dough.

Wincy's favourite riddle

What is green, has six legs and would kill you if it jumped out of a tree?
A snooker table.

Wincy's top favourite joke of all time

PILOT'S VOICE: *Ladies and gentlemen, we have just flown from London to Manchester in three minutes.*
PASSENGER: That must be a record.
PILOT'S VOICE: *No, this is the Captain speaking to you live.*

X's top twenty

X's favourite shaggy dog story

Some cowboys were sitting around a camp fire telling stories one evening. One of them said:

'I know an Indian chief who never forgets anything. The Devil can have my soul if I'm not telling the truth.'

That night the Devil appeared and said:

'I heard what you were saying tonight, and I'm ready to take your soul. Come along with me.'

'I was telling the truth,' said the cowboy. 'I'll show you.'

The two of them went to the Indian chief in the dead of night.

The Devil asked the Indian one question:

'Do you like eggs?'

'Yes,' the Indian chief replied.

Then the Devil and the cowboy went away. Twenty years later the Devil heard that the cowboy had died and, anxious to claim his soul, he went off to find the Indian.

'How!' the Devil said, greeting him Indian-style with his right arm raised.

'Scrambled,' answered the Indian.

X's favourite wisecrack

'It's a known fact that a tiger will not harm you if you carry a white stick.'
'Yes, but how fast do you have to carry the white stick?'

X's favourite knock knock

Knock, knock.
Who's there?
X.
X who?
Xtremely nice to see you again.

X's favourite animal joke

Which animal has antlers and wears white gloves?
Mickey Moose.

X's favourite potty poem

Little Miss Muffet sat on her tuffet,
Eating her curds and whey,
When along came a spider
Who sat down beside her
And said, 'Too much cholesterol, I'd say!'

X's favourite doctor doctor joke

DOCTOR: *'And what seems to be the trouble?'*
PATIENT: 'I get this feeling that nobody can hear what I'm saying.'
DOCTOR: 'I said, what seems to be the trouble?'

X's favourite monster joke

Why did the monster give up boxing?
He didn't want to spoil his looks.

X's favourite waiter waiter joke

'We have practically everything on the menu, sir.'
'So I see. Bring me a clean one.'

X's favourite daft definition

ABUNDANCE – A disco in a bakery.

X's favourite graffiti

*I NEVER KNOW WHAT TO BUY FOR
DINNER ANY MORE*
Kick the shelf at Tesco's and take what falls off.

X's favourite limerick

A cannibal bold of Penzance
Ate an uncle and two of his aunts,
A cow and her calf,
An ox and a half –
And now he can't button his pants.

X's favourite elephant joke

*How can you tell if an elephant has been in your
     bedroom?*
By the wrinkled sheets and the smell of peanuts.

X's favourite ghost joke

*What did X say when he saw the ghost of King
     Charles I?*
'You must be off your head!'

X's favourite school joke

Matilda was finishing her prayers.

'God bless Mummy and Daddy, and please
make Venice the capital of Italy.'

Her mother overheard this.

'Why did you say that?' she asked.

'Because,' explained Matilda, 'that's what I
put in my exam paper.'

X's favourite family joke

MRS A.: *What's your son doing these days?*
MRS B.: Cecil is at Medical School.
MRS A.: *What's he studying?*
MRS B.: He's not studying anything – they're
     studying him.

X's favourite funny book title

Round the Mountain by Sheila B. Cummin

X's favourite misprint

'Once again the committee thank Mr Amos Hope for his continuing help in cutting the churchyard grass. He said that his work had been made easier by people tidying up their own graves.'

Parish magazine

X's favourite pun joke

How do you use an Egyptian door bell?
Toot-and-come-in.

X's favourite riddle

What is hot and tasty and found in the jungle?
Snake and pigmy pie.

X's top favourite joke of all time

'I've just been out hunting. I caught five rabbits and a potfer.'
'What's a potfer?'
'To cook the rabbits in.'

Yvonne's top twenty

Yvonne's favourite shaggy dog story

A young man left university and got his first job as a door-to-door salesman, selling encyclopaedias. He went from house to house all day without making one single sale. Very depressed, he went to the last house on his list and a woman opened the door.

The young man, in a burst of enthusiasm, gave his sales talk about the encyclopaedias:

'. . . they are a mine of information, with all you need to know on cookery, gardening, history, politics, insurance, physics, chemistry, geography, and even psychology. There are twenty-four leatherbound volumes, each with 1,500 pages, which makes it three inches thick . . .'

'Hang on a moment,' said the woman and went inside and closed the door. After a couple of minutes she returned and said:

'I'll take Volumes One and Two.'

'Why only One and Two,' asked the young man, looking puzzled. 'Why not all twenty-four volumes?'

'Because the broken leg of our table is only six inches short.'

Yvonne's favourite wisecrack

'I just met a man I haven't seen for over ten years.'
'That's nothing. I just met someone I never saw
  before in my whole life.'

Yvonne's favourite knock knock

Knock, knock.
Who's there?
Yvonne.
Yvonne who?
Yvonne to be alone.

Yvonne's favourite animal joke

What family does the walrus belong to?
Don't ask me – no family in my street ever had a
  walrus.

Yvonne's favourite monster joke

*What did the monster eat after his teeth were
  pulled out?*
The dentist.

Yvonne's favourite potty poem

The rain makes all things beautiful,
The grass and flowers too.
If rain makes all things beautiful
Why don't it rain on you?

Yvonne's favourite doctor doctor joke

'Doctor, doctor, I've got a bad liver. What shall I
  do?'
'Take it back to the butcher immediately.'

Yvonne's favourite daft definition

GUILLOTINE – Something that gives you a pain in the neck.

Yvonne's favourite waiter waiter joke

'Waiter, waiter, there's a dead beetle in my wine.'
'You asked for something with a little body in it, sir.'

Yvonne's favourite graffiti

I HAVE TROUBLE CATCHING GROUSE
You're not throwing your dog up high enough.

Yvonne's favourite limerick

Maria, a sweet little miss,
Believed roller skating was bliss.
But she knew not her fate
For a wheel off her skate
Flew off and she landed like this!

Yvonne's favourite elephant joke

A woman sat on a bus eating peanuts. Trying to be friendly, she offered some to the woman sitting next to her.

'Good gracious, no!' said the woman, 'peanuts are so fattening.'

'What makes you think they are fattening?' asked the first woman.

'My dear,' said the second, 'have you ever seen a slim elephant?'

Yvonne's favourite ghost joke

How does a ghost look when it is worried?
Very grave.

Yvonne's favourite school joke

MOTHER: *How were your exams at school today?*
YVONNE: Oh, the questions were easy. It was the answers that I had a bit of a problem with.

Yvonne's favourite family joke

FATHER: *Neville, you are a pig! Do you know what a pig is?*
NEVILLE: Yes, it's a hog's little boy.

Yvonne's favourite funny book title

How I Crossed the Desert by Rhoda Camel

Yvonne's favourite misprint

'Mrs Noakes wore a black dress with a white lace front and she screwed up her face in a mischievous smile as her daughter Noreen pinned a rose to it!'

Enfield Gazette

Yvonne's favourite pun joke

'Do you like Chopin?'
'No, I get tired walking from store to store.'

Yvonne's favourite riddle

Why is Prince Charles like a cloudy day?
Because he is likely to reign.

Yvonne's favourite joke of all time

Did you hear about the man who was so unlucky, he broke his leg in an ear, nose and throat hospital?

Zeno's top twenty

Zeno's favourite shaggy dog story

At a fairground there was a stall at which you could throw darts, and if you scored a certain number of points you won a prize. This was a very popular attraction, and many people tried to win a prize and failed.

One man, however, came along and scored more than double the score needed to win a prize.

'Well done,' said the lady running the stall. 'You've won a prize. Here it is.'

She gave him a tortoise. The man looked quite pleased with this and off he went. About ten minutes later he appeared at the stall again, paid his money and was given three darts as before.

He aimed them at the dartboard and, to the lady's astonishment, he scored even more points.

'You *are* good at this,' she said. 'You've won another prize. What would you like this time?'

'Oh,' said the man, 'just give me another one of those crusty meat pies.'

Zeno's favourite wisecrack

People who view the world through rose-coloured spectacles end up by seeing red.

Zeno's favourite knock knock

Knock, knock.
Who's there?
Zeno.
Zeno who?
Zeno very well who's knocking!

Zeno's favourite animal joke

How do rabbits and hares make beer?
They start with hops.

Zeno's favourite monster joke

What goes out only at night and goes 'Chomp,
suck . . . ouch!'
A vampire with a rotten fang.

Zeno's favourite potty poem

During dinner at the Ritz
Father kept on having fits,
But something made me really ill –
I was left to pay the bill.

Zeno's favourite doctor doctor joke

'Doctor, doctor, what's the best way to stop my
      nose running?'
'Stand on your head.'

Zeno's favourite waiter waiter joke

'Waiter, waiter, you've got your thumb in my
      soup.'
'Don't worry, sir – it's not hot.'

Zeno's favourite daft definition

ZINC – Where you wash the zaucpans.

Zeno's favourite graffiti

*A SCHOOL REPORT IS A POISON PEN
LETTER WRITTEN BY TEACHER*

Zeno's favourite limerick

A well-built old fellow named Skinner
Said, 'How I do wish I were thinner!'
He lived for three weeks
On a grape and two leeks –
We think of him Sundays at dinner.

Zeno's favourite elephant joke

How can you tell if an elephant is under the bed?
Your head hits the ceiling.

Zeno's favourite ghost joke

Why are ghosts such simple things?
Because you can always see through them.

Zeno's favourite school joke

TEACHER: *Who shot Abraham Lincoln? Can you tell me, Zeno?*
ZENO: I'm not going to, Miss.
TEACHER: *Why ever not, if you know who did it?*
ZENO: Because I don't split on anybody.

Zeno's favourite family joke

BOY: *Mum, am I made of sage and onion?*
MOTHER: No, dear, of course you're not. Why?
BOY: *There's a boy in my class who says he's going to knock the stuffing out of me tomorrow.*

Zeno's favourite funny book title

The Long Walk Home by Miss D. Bus

Zeno's favourite misprint

'When you have switched the equipment off you are ready to connect up the wires. DO NOT connect the wife between A and B or you may get a nasty shock.'

Electrical magazine

Zeno's favourite pun joke

In a newspaper a reporter described the dress an Indian lady was wearing as a sarong instead of a sari. The next day he was made to write an apology for this error. His correction read:
    'What can I say except sari I was sarong.'

Zeno's favourite riddle

What would you do with a horse chestnut?
Take it to a throat specialist.

Zeno's top favourite joke of all time

WOMAN: *Hello, I believe you found a man's body in the Thames yesterday and he hasn't been identified?*

POLICEMAN: That's correct, madam. Why?

WOMAN: *My husband disappeared last week and I haven't seen him since. I wondered if it could be him.*

POLICEMAN: Can you tell me anything about your husband which might help us identify the body?

WOMAN: *Yes, he's cross-eyed and has a Scottish accent.*